INTRODUCTION

Everyone blushes. It's part of human nature.

However, some people blush more than others. Multiple factors, multiple causes but always the same consequences: a feeling of loneliness, of hopelessness over something that seems uncontrollable.

Some of us even develop a fear out of it, called Erythrophobia.

A lot has already been said and written about this condition that is now widely recognized and acknowledged in western medical literature.

This book will try to take a very practical approach by offering some of the best tips, tricks and treatments to reduce or cover facial redness.

By Fyfdpy.

Why do we blush
(and some more than others)?

Given a stimulus such as embarrassment or exercising, the person's sympathetic nervous system will cause blood vessels to open wide, flooding the skin with blood and resulting in reddening of the face.

The facial skin has more capillary loops per unit area and generally more vessels per unit volume than other skin areas. In addition, blood vessels of the cheek are wider in diameter, are nearer the surface, and visibility is less diminished by tissue fluid.

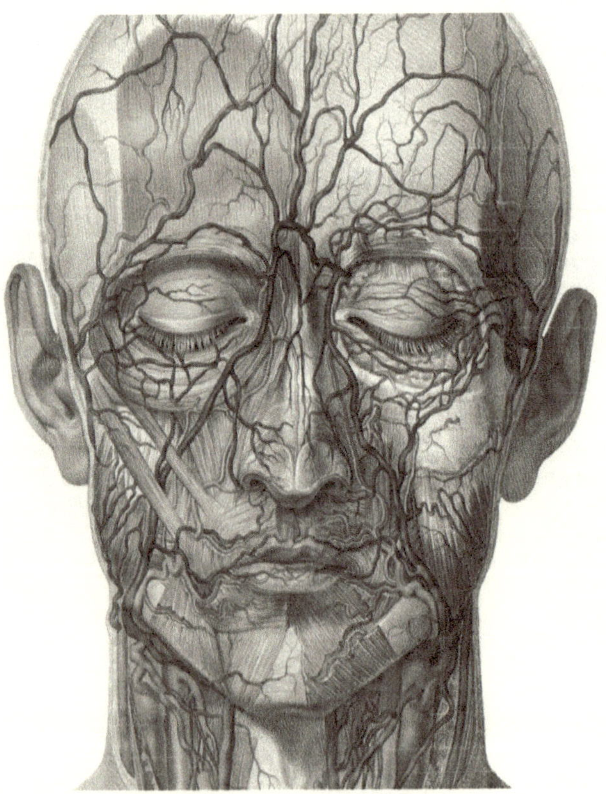

Blushing occurs when the tiniest blood vessels in your face, the capillaries, suddenly get wider. When they widen, more blood flows through them, which gives your skin a reddened, rosy appearance.

Blushing tends to occur only on the face, because there are more capillaries below the skin of the face than elsewhere and they're closer to the surface. So any signal to all the capillaries in your body to widen will make itself visible most often in your face.

That may explain why people blush only in their faces. However, it doesn't explain why some people blush more easily. Such people don't have more capillaries under the skin of their face than people who rarely blush.

It's possible that "blushers" have capillaries that dilate more easily in response to emotion or physical effort compared with people who blush less often. And blushing may be more obvious in some people, like those with fair skin, than in others.

Adrenaline also causes your blood vessels to dilate (called vasodilation), in order to improve blood flow and oxygen delivery. This is the case with blushing. The veins in your face respond to a signal from the chemical transmitter adenylyl cyclase, which tells the veins to allow the adrenaline to do its magic. As a result, the veins in your face dilate, allowing more blood to flow through them than usual, creating the reddened appearance that tells others you're embarrassed. In other words, adrenaline causes more local blood flow in your cheeks.

This sounds reasonable enough, but it's interesting to note that this is an unusual response from your veins. Other types of blood vessels are responsive to adrenaline, but veins generally aren't. In other regions of your body, veins don't do much when adrenaline is released; the hormone has little or no effect on them.

Blushing from embarrassment is a unique phenomenon. There are other means by which our cheeks become flushed: physical effort, drinking alcohol or becoming sexually aroused can cause us to blush, but only being embarrassed causes the type of blushing that is triggered by adrenaline.

Testimonial

"The best explanation I have received collectively after spending much time and money for many different doctors opinions is that I am perfectly healthy but for some unknown reason the blood vessels in my cheek area are either too close to the surface of the skin, during developmental stages there was some sort of blood vessel mutation that caused more than normal amount to be produced, or that the blood vessels themselves in that area are constantly dilated..."

Propranolol

Most people find it works right away, as in an hour or so after taking it. The standard dose for treating flushing is 10-40mg twice to three times a day.

1st testimonial

"After trying nearly everything on the market, I discovered a class of drugs known as beta-blockers. The one I was taking was **Propranolol**, 10 to 40mg a day as needed.

With some research, I found it to be the best for facial blushing.

Basically, without going into too much detail, **they slow your entire sympathetic nervous system down, and not only slow it down but it somehow keeps it there**.

Not only was I unable to blush, but my face was barely red at all since the medication also induces vasoconstriction.

But taking high blood pressure medication for someone with normal blood pressure is not a good situation. I felt nauseous for the rest of the day."

2nd testimonial

"I have been taking Propranolol for about three months now and it has DRAMATICALLY improved my flushing."

3rd testimonial

"It is not an ideal situation as Propranolol makes you lethargic and all. Are you on the lowest dose possible that still helps curb your flushing?"

4th testimonial

"Propranolol is a wonder drug - non-addictive and few side-effects. It saved my job, my sanity, my social life..."

5th testimonial

"I took 20mg about an hour before the ceremony, and I have never been so calm in my life. I wasn't even thinking about the crowd; I was cool, calm and collected."

6th testimonial

"My doctor prescribed 10mg Propranolol for the mild stage fright that I experience during public speaking. I usually split the pills and only take 5mg, which still reduces my physiological reactions."

7th testimonial

"I took a 40mg tab that evening, 2 hours before going out. Within an hour, I felt so relaxed, I literally felt my worries and anxiety were releasing from my body. Certain situations which would cause my anxiety to rise just didn't faze me all day long. I was proactive to try to provoke situations that could cause me to be anxious and nothing happened."

8th testimonial

"For me, it's been 3 and a half months now, and NOT ONE SINGLE BLUSH!!!"

9th testimonial

"I have been taking Propranolol for about three months now, and it has DRAMATICALLY improved my flushing, which is kind of puzzling to me because my greatest flushing trigger was a change in cold (or even just a tad chilly) weather to a warmer climate.

I also experienced anxiety-flushing, although it was much more transient, more like blushing. The cold weather flushing, however, was the classic ten-hour-long burning, pain flushing."

10th testimonial

"So when I began propranolol, i assumed only the anxiety flushing would be helped out. Much to my surprise, I have not flushed at all since being on propranolol. I can't say that I haven't turned red or anything, but the bright red, burning flush, the kind that everyone asks me if I'm okay and need to see a doctor, haven't had it at all. It was nothing short of shocking to me."

"I started using propranolol 5 years ago (early 20s) and noticed immediately that it helped not only with my social anxiety but also my rosacea."

Alcohol

There is one constant about drinking alcohol: it dilates the blood vessels in your body. That can result in numerous effects, some visible and some not.

Indeed, alcohol is a vasodilator. This allows more blood to the surface of the skin. The blood is hotter than the surface of your skin, so the receptors in your skin register this heat and you feel warm. Your face is especially capable of this because of its inbuilt mechanism of being able to blush.

Yet, for some people, their face will turn white after drinking. As their vessels dilate, gravity causes more blood to descend to the vessels below. As so much of it accumulates in their lower torso and legs, there is less to supply their face.

Thus, their face becomes pale because the subcutaneous capillaries are drained of the red blood which usually makes their facial skin look pink.

At intoxicating levels, alcohol is a vasodilator (it causes blood vessels to relax and widen), but at even higher levels, it becomes a vasoconstrictor, shrinking the vessels and increasing blood pressure.

Testimonial

Although a common trigger for rosacea, alcohol doesn't seem to be a problem for me. Weirdly, I become very pale when I drink.

7-11 breathing

Research suggest that when practiced consistently, controlled breathing will result in lower blood pressure and heart rate, which in turn results in less wear and tear on blood vessels. The vagus nerve plays a key role in this response.

The means by which controlled breathing triggers the parasympathetic nervous system is linked to stimulation of the vagus nerve - a nerve running from the base of the brain to the abdomen, responsible for mediating nervous system responses and lowering heart rate, among other things.

<u>The secret to stop blushing is to make use of your parasympathetic nervous system, and allow it to dampen the overactive sympathetic nervous system</u>.

The simplest method for enabling your parasympathetic nervous system to lower anxiety is to use 7-11 breathing.

This means that you **breathe in for a count of 7, hold briefly, and breathe out gently for a count of 11**.

No matter if you stick with the 7-11 count or some other combination, <u>make sure the out-breath is longer than the in-breath</u>.

The outward count expels the majority of the air from your body, something that doesn't happen often as most of us breathe in a very shallow way.

When your body gets enough oxygen, your heart rate and blood pressure slow down and become more regular.

Take a deep breath in through your nose for seven seconds. Then slowly exhale through your nose for 11 seconds. Some people have trouble breathing and exhaling for this long, so if you struggle, gradually build up; you can start at inhaling for two seconds and exhaling for five seconds, for example. Your goal should simply be to exhale for longer than you inhale. Your stomach should move out when you inhale; this is called diaphragm breathing, and is the most efficient way to breathe, according to the Cleveland Clinic.

Your breathing is like the holy grail to reducing anxiety and blushing, because when you breathe deeply, it will begin to stop all the other stress-related physical symptoms.

Whenever you know that you're about to face a stressful or challenging situation that causes you anxiety or stress, spend a few minutes before doing some deep slow rhythmic breathing.

Count in for seven, pause for the count of three and then breathe out for eleven seconds. By regularly doing this, you will train yourself to relax and condition yourself that the forthcoming stressful situations are safe.

You can do this any time you are put under pressure or you're anticipating something bad happening as you will be conditioning yourself to associate the situation as being safe.

Exhaling

Have you been exercising, or even texting, and notice you're holding your breath?

Sometimes our breathing changes in anticipation or while holding in a difficult emotion.

Essentially, breathing is a response to our activity and state of mind.

When we notice a lack of breath, the common response is to inhale and take a deep, forced breath.

The diaphragm is a dome-shaped muscle that rises to get the air out of the lungs as you breathe out.

Then, it moves down to make room for the air as you breathe in.

It's a common thought that inhaling is the important phase in the act of breathing, and people try to control it.

But this controlled inhale can actually place unhealthy pressure on the diaphragm, often tensing neck and chest muscles that do not need to be overly involved in breathing.

Because most people are busy taking an in-breath, they do not pay much attention to the exhale process. Without exhaling completely, excess carbon dioxide - a known stressor in your nervous system - may remain in your lungs.

The system detects that there is too much carbon dioxide and not enough oxygen.

Then, it does the only thing it know how to do: ask for more oxygen, causing another inhale.

Since the lungs are still partially filled with carbon dioxide, not as much oxygen can get in.

A cycle is set in motion and you keep inhaling for more oxygen, but can't get enough because the lungs have not been properly emptied. This habit can lead to shallow breathing and holding your breath.

However, when you exhale completely, your body is designed to take a "reflex" inhale.

Optimal breath means you do not suck air in to "take" a breath or "push" air out to expel a breath. You allow air to flow in and out, so the lungs easily exhale carbon dioxide and effortlessly fill with oxygen.

As your whole system slightly expands and contracts, your nervous system has the potential to settle and reduce stress.

Let your breath find its own rhythm. **Nothing is as close to you as your own breath. Some breaths may be long and deep, and others shorter. Like the ocean waves, flowing in and out, all breaths are not the same**.

The optimal breath brings fresh new oxygen to fill your whole torso and spread throughout your body to enhance life force. Then you can be present and able to engage in your next activity with full body, mind, spirit... and breath!

Follow one simple rule - exhale for double the amount of time you inhale.

Put simply, if you breathe in and count to four seconds, you should then slowly exhale and count to eight seconds as you do it.

This triggers a change in the nervous system from "sympathetic" mode - which is what we associate with fight or flight - to "parasympathetic" or "rest and digest" mode.

During times of stress, the nervous system becomes over stimulated leading to an imbalance.

Exhaling for twice as long as inhaling replicates the body's natural breathing when resting and fools the body and brain into being more relaxed.

By following this technique, it slows down the heart rate and relaxes the muscles, similar to when the body rests or sleeps and ultimately restores calm.

(Belly) breathing

You truly need to master your breathing because with anxiety always comes shallow or disrupted breathing. Your body is always affected when it comes to anxiety, so do not ignore that fact and only think to focus on what is going on in your head, for your body grows habits after being subjected to anxiety for such a time.

- When you inhale, you should feel the air also drift through the roof of your mouth almost tasting it, so that it goes all the way down into your lungs (you will feel this air in colder temperatures). I'm literally just saying that when you breathe, you should also feel the air sort of in your mouth even though you're breathing through your nose.

- **Your stomach should expand as you inhale, and it should naturally be relaxed (the tension of your abdomen is a sign of anxiety. We tend to involuntarily hold our breath too, you should get rid of such habit.)**

- **You want the switch from inhalation and exhalation to be fluid, no gaps.**

- **When you exhale your stomach should become relaxed, not back to being tense**.

- **The time between inhalation and exhalation should be as if you've just been running/exercising. Think of it as blowing air into a balloon. So breathe in.... let it go. Breathe in.... let it go. Breathe in.... let it go. Don't push your exhalation out, simply let it out**.

- Your body should start to tingle and you may get a little light headed (make sure you do not hyperventilate, stay in control of your breathing rate). You may start feeling euphoric and begin to be more self-aware and less self-conscious. This is the encouraging effect.

This breathing technique requires all your focus, which is why breathing is so important and effective during meditation, all your thoughts are forced to be cleared of your mind. That is because breathing affects everything in your body and energy is required for it to happen. **You may find that you keep going back to your habitual manner of breathing and you may start thinking that breathing techniques are ineffective. That is because you are not remaining focused long enough**. The more you practice this and perform NO other tasks, you will realize that you can literally think of nothing because of your complete focus on breathing.

You may zone back into your thoughts now and then, but that will actually make you realize that breathing this way makes you live in the moment instead of worrying about an uncertain/unlikely future and that the thoughts don't even affect you anymore because they no longer disrupt your breathing or body. When your mind is focused on consciously breathing, after practicing it for a long period of time, it will transition to it being subconscious and will naturally disrupt your negative thoughts the same way those thoughts used to disrupt your breathing and the function of your body due to constant pausing and losing focus. Our thoughts disrupt our physiology, which is why we shouldn't just think about changing thoughts but also about changing our disruptive bodily habits.

1st testimonial

"Well the other day I was looking in the mirror and noticed that my face would get redder during the day than when I would freshly wake up. So I spent about 10 minutes thinking about what could make my cheeks less red during the day and I figured it out. It's your breathing. During the night, we breathe full complete breaths and in my case I noticed that during the day i would only breathe in the minimal amount of air and I would sometimes hold my breath for a few seconds without knowing it.

So 2 days ago, I remembered my discovery and I started taking deeper breaths and tried to make the breaths last longer and after about 2 hours of doing this throughout my daily routine I noticed that a lot of my redness had subsided.

The next day, I breathed normally like I always do and the redness was back. So for me the amount of air I breathe in is related to the redness on my cheeks.

The only problem is that I've been breathing with short breaths for so long that I forget to breathe in deep breathes and I just get red cheeks again. So my question is do you guys see any difference in redness after hours of deep breathing or sleep, or is it just me?"

2nd testimonial

"Well basically when I go to bed I wake up in the morning and my face is pretty much normal. It's at a level that would be acceptable to me. However, like you as the day progresses it gets redder so I'm thinking it does have something to do with stress. Whilst sleeping your breathing is relaxed and at a constant balanced level. However, whilst awake during the day your breathing can be erratic, for instance holding breaths for longer and more shallow breaths too. Also there are external stress factors such as embarrassment or anxiety. You don't experience this whilst asleep. My thinking was to order some stress/anxiety supplement to see if that works.

Furthermore, solely on the breathing aspect, if I breathe deeply 5-10 times my face is pretty much normal color. I've heard oxygen is an alkaline rather than acidic. Therefore it is neutralizing our acidic blood level, thus affecting the redness of the skin."

3rd testimonial

"When I feel my temperature rising (that's when I know I'm going to get red) I start breathing through my mouth while I'm talking. I can't really explain it, and it probably makes no sense, but I've noticed it keeps me calmer and lowers my temperature/brings down my blushing."

4th testimonial

"Yes, I also noticed the lack of breathing due to stress. For instance today I had an interview and halfway through the manager told me to relax, he said my cheeks were bright red. Right then I realized that I had been talking a lot without breathing and then I would take really short breaths and hold it in.

After that I started breathing slow deep breaths and after the interview I looked in the mirror and my cheeks were practically normal. So the link between stress and the amount of breathing is definitely there. It's just so hard to constantly take big deep breaths when you're so used to just taking fast small breaths, I tend to forget easily and then the redness comes right back.

<u>I also noticed that the rest of my family (who has flawless skin by the way) always takes big deep breaths without even thinking about it and their face is always like porcelain</u>."

L-Theanine / GABA / Green tea

Cortisol, the stress hormone, can apparently accumulate in the blood stream during prolonged stress in some people and not others.

What reduces cortisol? L-Theanine, an amino acid found in high quality green Chinese/Japanese stewed tea.

Also possible to purchase L-Theanine as supplements, which are higher in mg than your cup of tea.

L-Theanine helps the body produce a neuroinhibitory neurotransmitter called GABA. When there are sufficient stores of GABA in the body, we can handle stress a whole lot better.

It doesn't make you drowsy or affect your memory like benzos.

Testimonial

"Within 2 days of drinking pints of cold green tea, my face and eyes were nearly normal, cold and white. One week later, I do not look as if I've ever had a problem."

Your imagination

Your imagination can directly influence every stirring of every molecule in your body. What you imagine can have an immediate effect on your body.

If you imagine something in the future that makes you nervous, your body reacts instantly by raising your blood pressure, increasing your breathing and pulse rates and giving you feelings of butterflies in your stomach. And all this from a split second of imagination.

Arnold Schwarzenegger sculpted his body in his mind through hypnotic visualization before producing the results for real. He also strongly visualized success in other areas in his life before achieving his goals in reality.

The phenomena of focused attention, imagery, biofeedback and therapeutic hypnosis all operate by altering the direction of blood flow. Altering blood flow by directed thinking, imagining and feeling is one of the basic, common factors in the resolution of most, if not all, mind-body problems.

Learn to redirect your blood flow: Blood is vital in our bodies. Not only does it ensure that every muscle and cell is nourished with oxygen and nutrients, but it also helps to ensure that life exists within an individual.

Blood flow in our bodies can be redirected through the use of imagination. For example, if you were to spend some time each day imagining that your legs or hands are around an open fire heating, you will be able to find out how easy you can redirect your blood flow.

When one blushes, blood rushes towards the face therefore making one to feel flushed around the cheeks and face. By redirecting your blood flow, you will be able to stop blushing effortlessly.

Blood flow

It is important to re-emphasize the importance of abnormal blood flow in rosacea. In one study, measurement of facial blood flow of rosacea sufferers compared to non-rosacea sufferers was off the charts.

Normal blood flow is very low and tightly controlled. An increase of resting blood flow by 2 times is incredibly high and pathologic. In microvascular physiology, this is so high that it would ensure damage to blood vessels and the dermis.

So, are the facial blood vessels really at fault, or is our body just pumping all of this blood into the face when we are not in a resting state? It would seem to me that the facial blood vessels are normal, but become damaged due to all the blood flow. Perhaps whatever is sending all this blood to the face in the first place is the real problem.

Each organ has its own mechanisms to control blood flow. So there can be normal blood flow throughout the rest of the body, but if the facial feed vessels open up, then just the face will have higher blood flow.

There was an article where they measured the forearm blood flow and found it normal, while the face's was outrageously high.

The sympathetic nervous system does control many organs, so when that is activated, many organs change their blood flow - some constrict and some dilate.

So how do we decrease blood flow to the face enough to stop the redness. Can we surgically cut off the feed vessels to the face, say, through the inner mouth, so that the outer facial skin is not scarred?

Testimonial

"My feet and hands are cold, but my face seems to get way too much blood flow and is often warm or hot (flushed). Is there a connection to rosacea? Or has anyone overcome their poor circulation?

Also, on a side note, any little bump, scratch or even touching of my skin causes localized redness.

If I press down on my hand and then let go, that part of my hand is let significantly whiter than the rest of my hand for a few seconds.

When I looked at it more closely, I saw that the skin on my face reacts very similarly to my hands. If I press on it and let go, it also leaves a clearly visible white spot that lasts for a few seconds.

I feel that my rosacea symptoms go hand in hand with my poor circulation.

<u>I feel that my face gets the majority of the blood flow in my body. It's funny to think that this is somehow restricting/limiting blood flow to other parts of the body</u>."

Acupressure

Acupressure is a manual procedure of rotary compression or thrust of your fingertips into known oriental acupuncture points, that stimulate or sedate the autonomic nervous system.

All that is needed is for you to stimulate your acupuncture points along the related meridians each day and several times a day. As your blood pressure fluctuates throughout the day, this will help to keep it under control.

The beauty of it is that it can be done anywhere, anytime, on your body.

Emergency techniques for lowering high blood pressure

We start at the carotid sinus that is located at the top of your Adam's apple where you will slide your fingers back until you feel a pulsation and lightly press on both sides of your neck. This gland regulates your blood pressure. Hold that area for a slow five-minute count inhaling deeply then exhaling. Repeat three times.

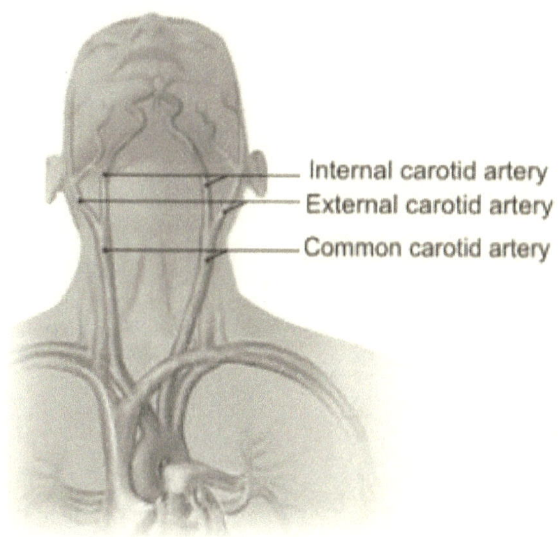

<u>Large Intestine LI 4</u>

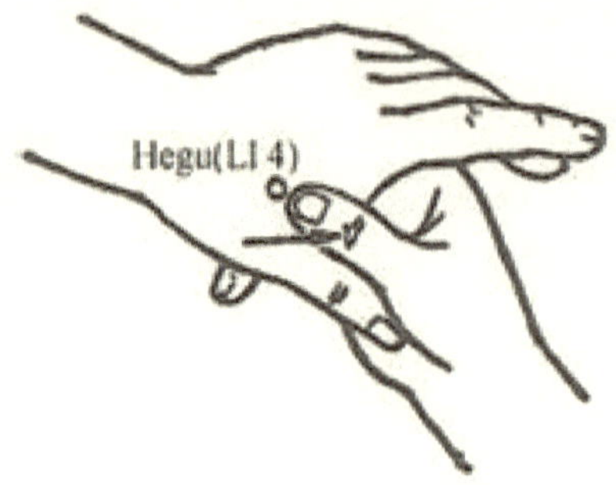

- Diseases of the head and face (*congestion, swelling, nasosinusitis, facial tic...*)
- Gastric pain, abdominal pain, constipation, diarrhea, dysentery.
- Use in conjunction with LIV 3 to strongly move the qi and blood in the body in order to remove stagnation and alleviate pain. It calms and balances blood flow throughout the body and clears stagnation.

<u>ST 36</u>

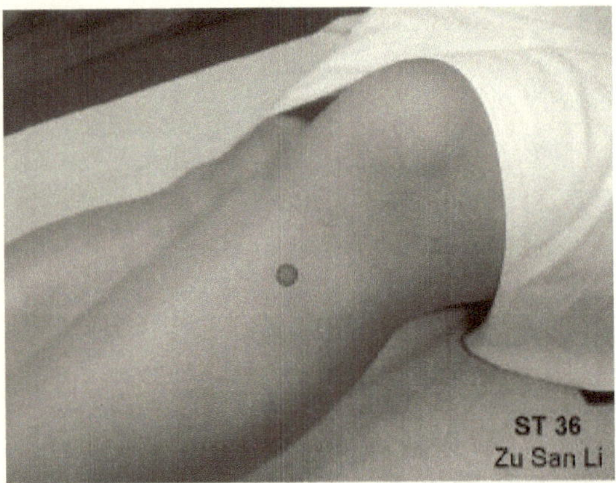

ST 36 or Stomach 36 is an effective acupressure point to treat hypertension, arteriosclerosis, and circulatory disorders. It rejuvenates the chi and blood and restores the balance of the energies. This point is called the Leg Three Miles, and it is positioned four finger widths below the lower edge of the kneecap and one finger width off the shin bone to the outer side.

<u>PC 6</u>

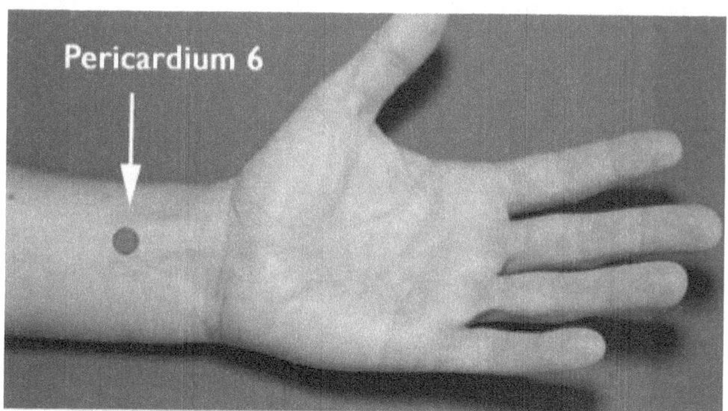

It is yet another important acupressure point for treating high blood pressure. It soothes and helps the heart and circulatory system in their proper functioning. It also helps to relieve anxiety, nausea, vomiting, motion sickness, chest congestion, etc.

The facial arteries can be compressed by exerting strong pressure at a point one inch in front of the angle of the lower jaw. These arteries pass over the jaw at these points. They should be pressed at the same time on both sides.

The common carotid artery can be reached at a point one and a half inches above the joint between the breastbone and the collar bone. Pressure may be exerted inward or backward (fig. 41).

The subclavian artery can be reached at a point behind the middle of the clavicle or collarbone where the hump of this bone is felt. First lower and draw the shoulder forward, then press downward and backward with the thumbs or with the fingertips of both hands. The pressure must be firm and persistent. (Fig 42.)

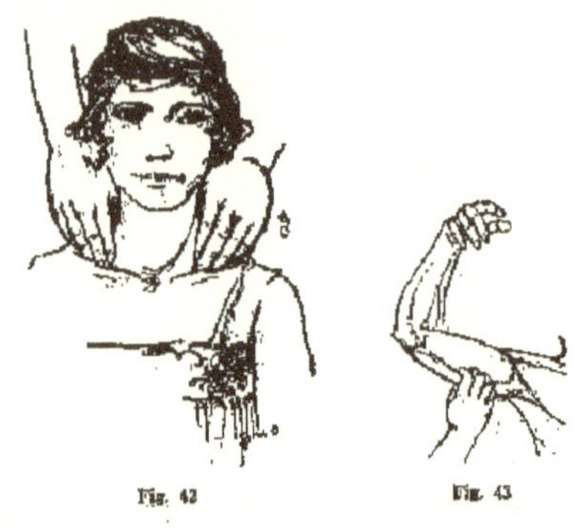

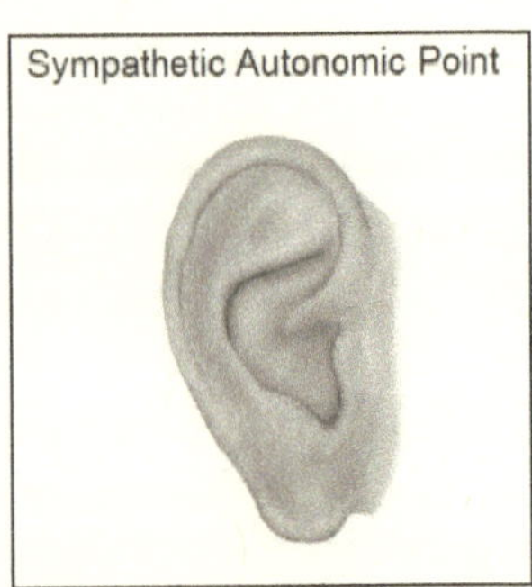

Do you remember learning about the Sympathetic versus the Parasympathetic nervous systems?

Too many people choose to live in a constant sympathetic nervous system state. The sympathetic nervous system was designed to jumpstart our bodies into fight or flight mode for survival purposes. Basically, our digestive and organ functions shut down so that we can save ourselves during emergency situations.

Parasympathetic mode, on the other hand, is where we should be most of the time. This is where our body regenerates and heals. When someone comes in for acupuncture, it is our responsibility to help him or her to move back into parasympathetic function. The Sympathetic Autonomic Point will do exactly that.

Located on the inner part of the helix, massaging this point on the ear helps to calm the body's "fight-or-flight" response, designed to prompt us into action and pump adrenaline throughout our bodies in the face of danger. However, in modern society, many people unfortunately live in a constant state of fear and stress, because their sympathetic nervous system is simply overwhelmed and overstimulated.

Simply put, we do not give our bodies and minds near enough self-care and time to decompress as we should, which means that our systems have to work that much harder in order to maintain functionality. However, giving attention to this part of your ear can give your body and mind a chance to restore itself and heal from all the stresses you face each day.

Massaging this point on your ear also helps instill a regular heartbeat, eliminate stress, relax the muscles, and bring the nervous system back into a state of tranquility.

Arterial supply of the face

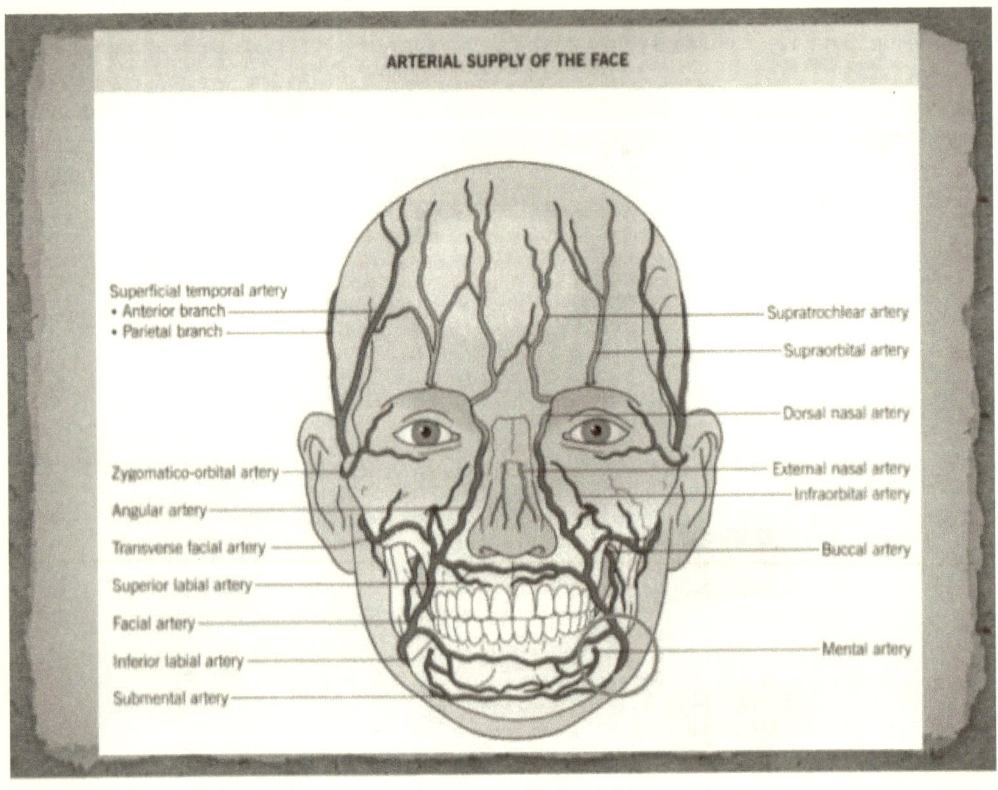

Supra-Orbital Artery
Zygomaticotemporal Branch of Zygomatic Nerve
Temporal Branches of Facial Nerve
Superficial Temporal Artery Parietal Branch-
Frontal Branch-
Auriculotemporal Nerve
Middle Temporal Vein
(Palpebral Branch) of Lacrimal Nerve
Superficial Temporal Vein
Superficial Temporal Artery
Zygomatic Branches of Facial Nerve [VII]
Transverse Facial Artery
Parotid Plexus
Facial Nerve [VII] Cervical Branch - Marginal Mandibular Branch-
Posterior Auricular Vein
External Jugular
Supratrochlear Artery
Medial and Lateral Branches of Supra-Orbital Nerve
Supratrochlear Vein
Supratrochlear Nerve
Infratrochlear Nerve
External Nasal Nerve (of Anterior Ethmoidal Nerve)
Angular Artery
Zygomaticofacial Branch of Zygomatic Nerve
Infra-Orbital Artery
Inferior Palpebral Branches of Infra-Orbital Nerve
Superior Labial Branches of Infra-Orbital Nerve
Buccal Nerve
Buccal Branches of Facial Nerve [VII]
Superopr Labial Branch of Facial Artery
Cutaneous Branch
Facial Vein (Angular Vein)
Inferior Labial Branch of Facial Artery
Mental nerve
Mental Branch of Inferior Alveolar Artery
©KevinCease
KevinCease.com

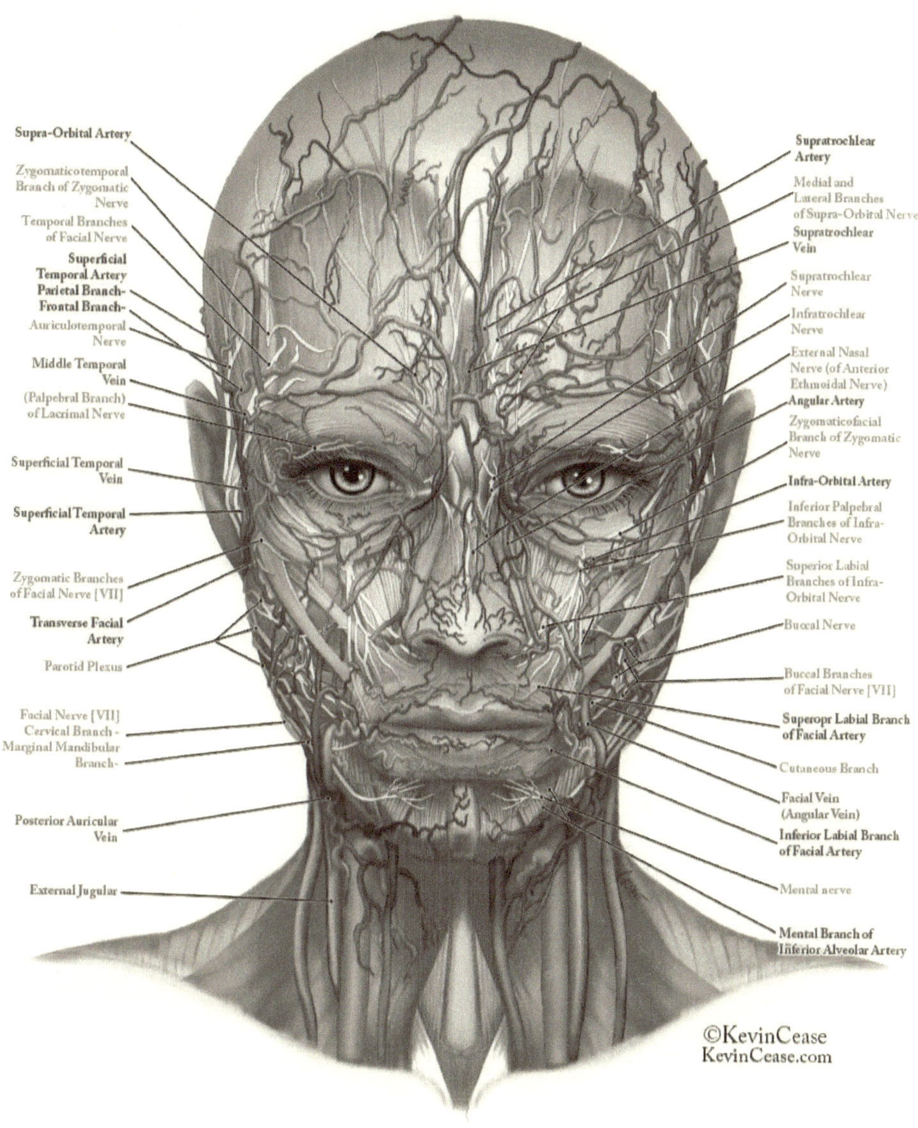

25

Superficial arteries and veins of face and scalp

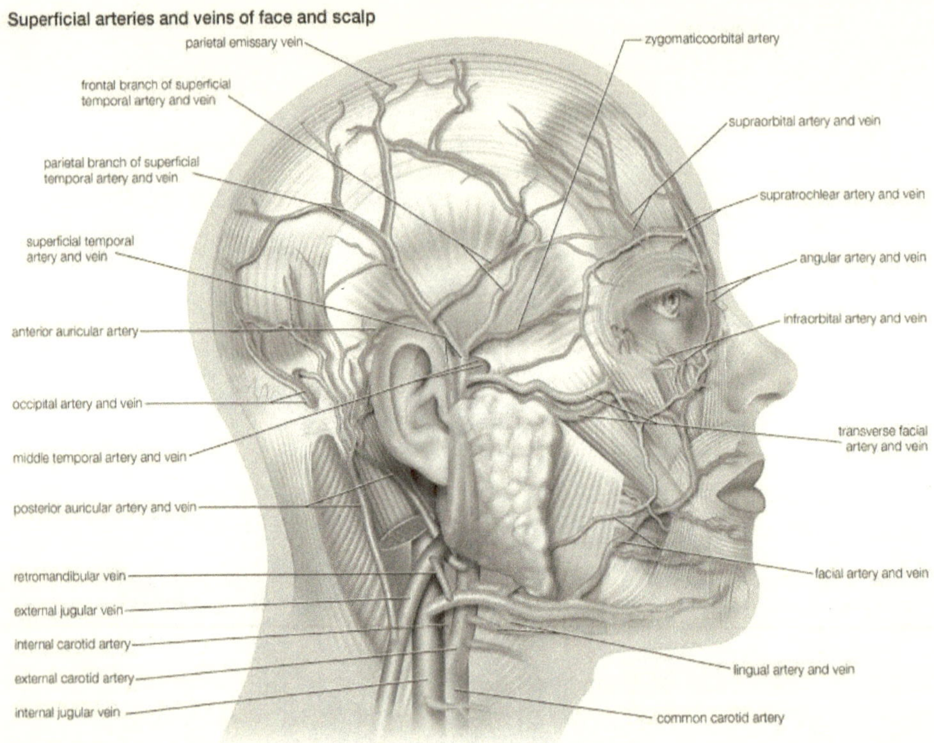

Physical vs. Mental

I believe some blushers are 100% mental and some flushers may be 100% physical. I believe my blushing is a bit of both. While a lot can be controlled mentally, not all of it can.

For example, when I exercise or come in from hot/cold temperatures or cough, that is not "all in my head". That is a physical response, which tells me that there is something off with my body.

Testimonial

"For me I keep coming back to the physical aspect about how the skin is different from person to person, and then specifically about how many blood capillaries people have in the outer skin in the face. Most people I find are not able to blush no matter what (or being able to get flushing of the face for that matter), simply because they do not have blood capillaries in the face that can be visible when expanded. I am not excluding the impact the nervous system has, btw. It definitely has an impact on facial blushing. When you blush, it is because the sympathetic nervous system is active, and that process you have no control over.

My argument is just this: everyone has a sympathetic nervous system that gets active, for example when you get embarrassed. Who blushes or not, and how badly it is, depends on the amount of blood capillaries in the face (and how far out in the face they are, etc.). The physical definition of facial blushing is just blood rushing to the capillaries so that they expand. No matter how overactive the nervous system is, if you do not have blood capillaries which expands, you simply are not able to blush. If someone has a different nervous system that sends more blood to the face than most people, I do not know. I don't think so, but then again I am not a doctor."

Sudafed / Pseudoephedrine

Basically, the pseudoephedrine is a vasoconstrictor which constricts the blood vessels in your face making it harder for them to open up (which happen when you blush).

1st testimonial

"I can completely eliminate facial flushing by taking **pseudoephedrine** in advance of a stressful and potential triggering event. This works for me every time and never failed me yet. Two **Sudafed** tablets last about 4 to 5 hours.

I am a very highly-paid executive and my magic bullet has helped me mask my problem to others in stressful meetings and many eye-to-eye contact meetings with high-power people."

2nd testimonial

"I was certainly surprised that Sudafed worked like that for me. In a nutshell, I still had some heart palpitations during social situations but no blushing and was able to speak in situations where I normally would not. Strange indeed."

3rd testimonial

"Today, I took the Sudafed about an hour before my presentation and did not flush once. I was nervous and anxious, messing up a few times with pronunciations but still, no flush. I even noticed my body's response to my anxious state when I was waiting for my turn to present, in which would usually result in flushing."

4th testimonial

"I take Sudafed (two tablets = 120 mg) from time to time and it really works great. There is no flushing for about 5 hours.

The skin returns to its normal state afterwards, there is no rebound effect."

5th testimonial

"It works, that much is for sure. I took four 30mg pills, the generic kind. I did my presentation, which took approximately 35 minutes, and didn't come close to flushing once."

6th testimonial

"I can say it was a success. No flush at all. The strange thing is it gave me some weird self-confidence boost. I rubbed my chest to see if it gets red easily like it always does and it stood pale.

After 6 hours, my head started to hurt a little bit - it felt like the blood pressure rose up."

Asian flush = they take a Sudafed an hour before drinking and it's pretty much cured.

Clenching your fist?

Testimonial

"A technique of vasoconstriction is by clenching my fist and transferring that action to another part, usually one that was bleeding. It works very well, I can feel the area tightening up, the bleeding slows and stops, and I then expand the tightening feeling further up the limb as I release my fist and then tighten it again.

I have been using the technique lately on my face as I find I have been getting redder and redder over the slightest things.

As soon as I feel the heat spread up into my face, I clench my fist, without being noticed, and tighten the skin on my face. It has made a big difference as I can feel the warmth slow down, and reduce quickly.

To train, I find a good time and place, and just try and get my face as pale as possible.

Basically the point of the exercise is that you focus on an area of your choice, and by squeezing your hand you imagine the squeezing action tightening the area. I should be able to just do it mentally, but haven't been able to. The brain must work better with a reference; the hand being squeezed.

To start out, concentrate on an area you have a good 'reference' to, such as your fingers, which you use all the time. If you can get the tightening feeling on your finger, you can move to another area such as your face. I found it difficult to start as I don't always have feeling, as such, from my face to focus on. But once it starts to feel warm, I can feel it better and it is more effective."

Massage

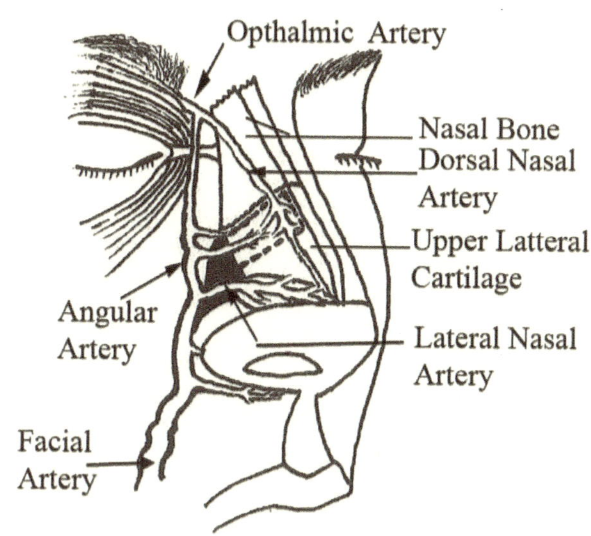

Buccal artery: Supplies blood to the cheeks

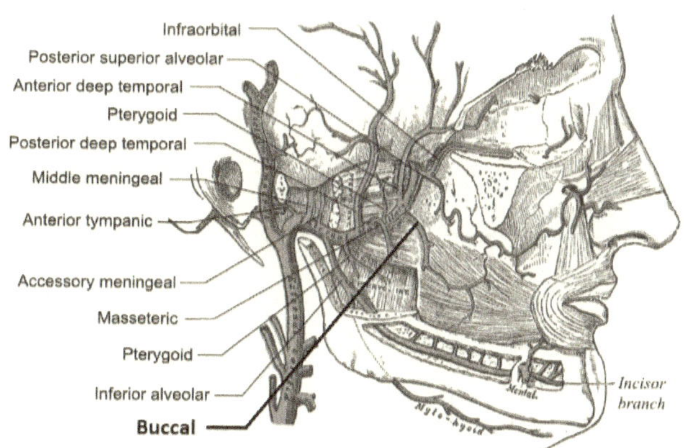

Mirvaso

MIRVASO® (brimonidine) topical gel, 0.33% is the first and only FDA-approved medication developed and indicated for the persistent (non-transient) facial redness of rosacea.

- Only a tiny drop mixed in with your daily face moisturizer.

- A very small amount, spread thinly.

- If you can still see paleness on day 2, do not add more to your face, wait until the effects have completely gone before using it again.

- After 2 hours of applying it, you can wash it off and still get the same good results and stay away from redness triggers (sun, alcohol…).

- The redness clears up all day.

1st testimonial

"I've found that by using a small amount of Mirvaso twice a week along with my usual skincare routine it has made a real difference."

2nd testimonial

"Let me repeat that I am using very small amounts of Mirvaso.

I literally add NO MORE THAN two or three drops from the tiny bottle to a rather large dollop of cream; I add a few drops of water to that, I stir it all around with my finger, and then I use that to paint my entire face."

> **Caution**: Rebound flushing has been pointed out with the cream Mirvaso, which contains brimonidine, an adrenergic agonist.

3rd testimonial

"My dermatologist advised me to proceed slowly with this gel, adding a small amount more per day to my regular rosacea moisturizer. Even a small amount immediately cleared up my redness for almost the whole day. I have been very happy with it. For anyone having problems, try this "go slow" method that my doctor told me about."

Stomach

When blushing, parallel to face, stomach blushes too.

Indeed, when you blush, the lining of your stomach also turns red. This is due to the sympathetic nervous system increasing blood flow throughout the body.

Here are my tips: if you feel yourself going red, try to relax and **purposefully stick your belly out**. Breathe deeply, and do not think about your redness. **Visualize your feet/legs (or anywhere that's covered up) going red or getting hot, and imagine your face is cold and pale. This can redirect the extra blood flow in your face (eg. blushing).**

What I find works is when you start to blush imagine that the blood is flowing to your feet and they are getting red, your feet get a little hot but it really works.

The more tense you get as you start to blush, the more the blood is forced to the face. One trick is, when you feel it coming on, to deliberately drop your shoulders, relax your body, and push your stomach out. This takes a bit of doing at first, so you might want to practice.

Testimonial

"I find that when my stomach is uneasy or have the butterflies that I'm instantly ready to blush. The worst thing is the instant blushing. The total adrenaline rush of blood within a second."

Water

Drink lots of water! A lot of times blushing occurs because of dehydration.

Dehydration can cause facial flushing, so drinking enough water is essential to prevent unwanted blushing.

Also, if you know you are going to have to make a speech, speak to people who intimidate you or meet with a person you fancy, you can prevent blushing for up to 30 minutes by drinking an icy bottle of water a few minutes before you enter the situation.

1st testimonial

"I used to blush all the time. Then I started really watching my water intake. I mean I became quite religious about drinking a glass of water every hour. I have not blushed since."

2nd testimonial

"I find a drink of cold water helps me - to be more specific, carrying a water bottle filled with COLD water and taking a nice big swig when you feel that blush coming on. It's not a 100% guarantee of a blush-free face, but I find it helps."

3rd testimonial

"I do want to share that I just talked to a girl who was chronically dehydrated and was hot all the time. The result of the heat was flushing and sweating. I imagine not sweating would make blushing even worse... but it's likely for someone to have both. I realized that for the longest time I drank SO MUCH WATER. But it would go straight through me, as if my body didn't absorb it. People made fun of me for how much I had to run to the bathroom. I've been doing some research, and apparently you can drink a lot of water every day and STILL be chronically dehydrated. Which results in blushing problems.

And this comes from not getting the electrolytes in your water that you need to help the cells absorb water. Think about getting some natural electrolyte tablets that are low in sugar and that are natural if you think heat is partly to blame. I believe that if our bodies have enough water, then they have the ability to stay cool in heated situations. My body has been doing so much better since I started drinking electrolytes and coconut juice!"

Bicarbonate soda / Antacid

Testimonial

"Hi everyone. I have some good news for you!!! I started blushing excessively in high school and it has become increasingly problematic. It has greatly affected me at work and socially. In fact it has made me quite socially phobic and I can't even talk on the phone without breaking into a sweat. In searching for an answer, I came across the most simple solution that is used by actors and performers who also suffer chronic blushing. Bicarbonate Soda. Simple as that.

You can swallow a teaspoon of bicarb soda with water before a meeting/performance/social engagement (whatever triggers you).

Or, as I have recently discovered, antacid (with sodium bicarbonate) works just as well. You can buy it at your local pharmacy and it is already in an easy chewable dose (although I think it taste disgusting and I still swallow with water). Just don't exceed the recommended dosage!

Antacid is very common and should be sold in every chemist anywhere in the world. It is used to treat indigestion. You don't need a prescription or anything. I think Mylanta is an international brand, but it doesn't matter what brand you buy, just check the pack to make sure it contains sodium bicarbonate (they don't all). I don't know exactly how long the effects last, but I think maybe 1-2 hours. But I just take one tablet once a day before I do something that will cause me to flare up.

The dosage on the pack is actually 2 tablets, 3 times a day (to treat indigestion). Don't be afraid to go to the chemist today and give this a try. At \$2 a pack, you have nothing to lose!"

Blood thinner

A woman was cured of flushing by taking a blood thinner for people, PLAVIX.

A neuroimmunologist found out (with a special blood test) that she suffered from a certain blood coagulation dysfunction. This causes that the blood cannot flow off the head accurate (microcirculation dysfunction). This has already been assumed as cause for rosacea from some scientists.

A daily aspirin (100mg) should have a similar function as Plavix. It blocks prostaglandin D1, which is considered one of the sources of inflammation in the body. One study suggests that aspirin can reduce flushing by 40%

Testimonial

"My dermatologist told me to take 500mg of aspirin a day to reduce intense facial flushing."

Tantien / Hara

We need to move from our heads and down to our center, which is called in Chinese TANTIEN, HARA in Japanese.

It is our abdominal-area, just below the navel.

Move your energy to your center. It goes to your head - okay. Try again. And again. Like in other training, continuity and effort is alpha-omega.

When you have no control of your energy, your energy goes to your head, when you feel stressed.

When you have control of your energy - your energy follows your mind, and you can keep it down in your center.

You do this by focusing, combined with abdominal-breathing.

You breath in through your nostrils, out through your mouth.

Your exhalation should take twice the amount of the time you use on your in-breath.

During this exercise, relax your body, and try not to force your breathing, but let it become natural and relaxed.

In the beginning, it feels unnatural, but it will feel more and more natural, the more you practice.

Testimonial

"I feel that my will power increase but I still cannot control my blushing in these situations:
1) when I talk to people and look at people's eyes, blood start to surge towards my face area and I blush.
2) Or when someone walks up to me from behind out of a sudden, I will also blush.

Basically my blush kick starts itself when I stop breathing momentarily (talking too fast and shock/surprise)."

Vasoconstrictors

Cypress oil

Cypress Oil causes blood vessels to contract. This can be beneficial in cases of excess bleeding.

Smelling cypress oil can also cause blood vessels to constrict.

Cypress is an effective vasoconstrictor, which means it helps to narrow dilated blood vessels such as varicose veins or broken capillaries that appear on the face. Blend it with lemon or bitter orange together with Frankincense oil in a base cream or lotion for this type of application. **It also helps to balance oily skin when used in this way.**

Nasal Spray / Afrin / Oxymetazoline

Oxymetazoline and other constrictors work by binding the alpha 1 receptors on the capillaries, constricting the vasculature.

The trick is to apply oxymetazoline (for example, Afrin) nasal spray directly to the reddish areas twice daily. The vasoconstrictive action of the product can be helpful for suppressing the flush. **Unlike its use in the nose, which is restricted to three consecutive days, these products may be used on the face for extended periods of time without concern**.

Direct skin application with Afrin (or a generic equivalent) spray may offer few hours of redness camouflage with its vasoconstrictive effect.

1st testimonial

"If you are looking for a cooling gel the best I've tried is rubbing Afrin nasal decongestant on your face. It constricts the blood vessels for up to 8 hours and works quite well."

2nd testimonial

"For the past few weeks, in the morning, I have been rubbing a few drops of Afrin onto the areas of my face, neck and chest that tend to gradually flush. These days I have not flushed. It's a pretty significant finding for me actually. One day, I only put it on one side of my face and the side without Afrin did start to splotch when I was speaking in front of a group. I think I am onto something here!"

3rd testimonial

"I remember rubbing it to both sides of my face before I went to the pub one night. When I was in the pub and I had drank about 2 pints, I felt the flush coming on and as usual I turned into a hermit not talking to anyone as I was so self-conscious. I was sure the Afrin wasn't working.

Anyway, I then went to use the bathroom and when I was walking past the mirror, I noticed my face was completely pale. It was unbelievable really, it lasted for the whole night after drinking all night and when I got home I tried my hardest to make myself flush but only a slight flush came on.

I haven't used it as much since because my flushing has improved significantly but I always keep a bottle in my bag just in case."

> For anyone trying this remember the study used 0.05% oxymetazoline, so if this is the strength you buy and then you mix it with a lotion, you will be diluting it. Perhaps it is best to get some 0.1% and mix the entire contents thoroughly with the same amount of lotion.

4th testimonial

"I tried it again today. Results: Very impressive. ~50% reduction in redness."

5th testimonial

"So I used about twice as much of this stuff as I normally do, and the results were dramatic. Within an hour I was actually paler than normal, and the condition improved until I was ghostly pale after 2 hours.

I applied it at ~4 a.m. and the effect was still strong at 12:30 p.m., when I went to sleep.

Then I woke up at 5:00 p.m. and haven't noticed any rebound."

6th testimonial

"I love this stuff, but the application process seems to be important.

When I've applied it directly to my face, without any moisturizer, it doesn't seem to sink in too well, and I imagine most of it evaporating off my skin into the air.

That's why I apply some moisturizer (not sure if oil works the same, I use an Aloe Vera cream) and pat my face with a towel, so my skin has a tacky feel to it - not too much moisturizer, but just the right amount.

Also, I apply a lot of the oxymetazoline - probably a dozen sprays, at the least. For me, it takes about 4 sprays to get the pump primed - then it squirts out a large amount. And my most successful times were when there was a lot of white stuff in the liquid. That seems to be the active ingredient. For example this morning, I was getting down to the bottom of the bottle and it came out really thick and white. (Now that I think about it, if it's settling on the bottom then maybe I should be shaking it first... but anyway.)

I spray it in one palm first, then proceed to apply it. I tilt the bottle at different angles, whatever works to make it come out best. It's usually tilted downward. Sometimes I have to hold it upright to prime it, though.

Until I started using it every day for 10 days straight, I'd been using it occasionally with no problems. So, I think it can be done safely, but the price of experimentation can be very high if you get a bad result."

Caution: a lot of those who used a nasal spray in this way got serious and painful rebound flushing and reported that their skin was in worse shape after discontinuing use.

Phenylephrine

The main ingredient of Preparation H (hemorrhoid cream) is Phenylephrine. You might recognize the name because it is also found in common over-the-counter medications like decongestants, and decongestant nasal sprays.

Physicians use it because it is an alpha agonist, meaning it works through a receptor on a blood vessel to make the blood vessel constrict.

So, you can use it when blood vessels are too dilated to shrink them.

Redness diminishes greatly after instillation of topical phenylephrine (10%) because this vasoconstrictor has great effect on the superficial episcleral vessels.

The phenylephrine in hemorrhoidal cream is a potent constrictor and is used to constrict large veins and arteries. But it is so strong that it will cause rebound flushing.

"I have also tried topical phenylephrine in both 1 and 2%. It seems for me to be able to vasoconstrict more of the superficial flushing, but does little for the deep flushing if I have a trigger like heat. You can actually see the skin around the flush zone become quite pale, even compared to the normal tissue. If I'm not having a really deep flush, it can take it away completely. It doesn't have the same effects for extended periods of time though. I do notice that my face looks more pale and is less reactive at the end of the day when I use it. It sort of halts the hyperactivity cycle a bit. However, the skin doesn't seem to keep that striking paleness that it takes on when first applied for very long. I would say maybe 20-45 min only, and it certainly won't stop the deep flushing. Anyway these are just my experiences."

Peppermint oil

One of the most powerful vasoconstrictors in aromatherapy, peppermint oil is excellent for **cooling hot conditions like hot flash**, tired and achy legs, hands and feet…

German Chamomile essential oil

It has vasoconstrictor benefits.

Indeed, the oil extracted from the chamomile is credited with possessing vasoconstrictor properties that ultimately reduce the redness of skin that is brought on by the enlargement of blood capillaries.

Chamomile's healing properties do wonders. Its anti-inflammatory nature will soothe redness and itching, reduce swelling and heat associated with dermatitis and prevent inflammation and negative reactions due to irritating cosmetics. Its antiseptic qualities destroy bacteria, and the plant's anodyne - which is similar to an analgesic - relieves pain. The herb's vasoconstrictive abilities aid the narrowing and healing of unsightly facial capillaries.

Pranayama (Control of prana through breath)

Control of the Prana (vital life energy) leads to control of the mind. Yoga teaches breathing exercises called Pranayama, which means 'control of the Prana'.

All diseases of the body can be destroyed at the root by controlling and regulating the Prana, this is the secret knowledge of healing. However, most people only use a fraction of their lung capacity. They breathe shallowly barely expanding their ribcage. In ordinary breathing, we extract very little Prana. But when we concentrate and consciously regulate the breathing, we are able to store a greater amount.

What most of us need these days is a breathing program that can help us at our desks, cars and computers.

- Tension and even depression may be overcome by the following simple exercise.
- Place the shoulder blades as close together as you can without strain and exhale gently and fully
- Pause, then inhale with a deep, slow, gentle breath until the lungs are comfortably filled
- <u>Breathe out slowly through the nose with a long sigh and without altering the position of the shoulder blades</u>
- Do this a dozen times and depression will disappear

You will have stimulated the brain and eased nerve tension by providing a fuller supply of life-giving oxygen.

The person with abundant Pranic energy radiates vitality and strength, which can be felt by all coming into contact with her/him.

The Yogic Breath

- To get the feel of proper diaphragmatic breathing, wear loose clothing and lie on the back
- Place the hand on the upper abdomen, where the diaphragm is located
- Breathe in and out slowly
- The abdomen should expand outward as you inhale and contract as you exhale
- Breathe in slowly; expand the abdomen, then the ribcage and finally the upper portion of the lungs
- Then breathe out in the same manner, letting the abdomen cave in as you exhale
- This is the Complete Yogic Breath

Generally speaking, a good breath is one where you breathe in through the nose - deeply - from the diaphragm, filling your lungs with energizing oxygen, and then forcibly ejecting the waste product carbon dioxide as your lungs deflate.

Many people tend to be shallow mouth breathers, heaving their chests in and out as they take in less oxygen than they need, and getting rid of less CO_2 than they should.

This can lead to feeling lethargic, unfocused, and stressed out. You may not realize just how much your breathing affects your nervous system's responses to outside stressors.

When you breathe deeply through your nose, it's like an 'off' switch for your sympathetic nervous system. It activates your parasympathetic nervous system and tells your body to relax and recuperate.

<u>Set a reminder a few times each day to simply "check in" with your breathing. Put one hand on your chest and the other on your belly and breathe for a few minutes. The focus here is to simply remind yourself to breathe in through your nose and deep into your belly</u>. You should feel your belly rise and fall with little movement in your chest (it helps to maintain good posture while doing this - a nice side effect).

Another breathing technique is known as Box Breathing. It gets its name from the cycle of breathing in, holding, breathing out, and holding for the same count. To practice, get into a comfortable position and then begin inhaling deeply through your nose as your count (*starting with a four-count is usually the best*). Inhale as you count to four, and then hold as you count to four, so your lungs take full advantage of the next oxygen inside them. Then, exhale through a slightly open mouth as you count to four. Finally, with your lungs emptied out, count to four before beginning the cycle again with an inhale. This is an incredibly centering way to breathe, and it can help you prepare for anything from a tough workout to a stressful meeting.

MAGNESIUM + VB6

Magnesium is a bit of a wonder vitamin. It's critical for almost 300+ bodily functions and reactions. One of its major effects though is that it is a relaxant.

That's why you could see a marked decrease in your blushing by taking it.

Liver

It has been found by scientists that the liver blushes at the same time as the face blushes. So when the face begins to blush, all one has to do is concentrate on the position of the liver and it then blushes instead of the face. With a little practice, this method becomes very easy.

The diagram below shows the position of the liver for the sufferer to concentrate on. It is on the right hand side.

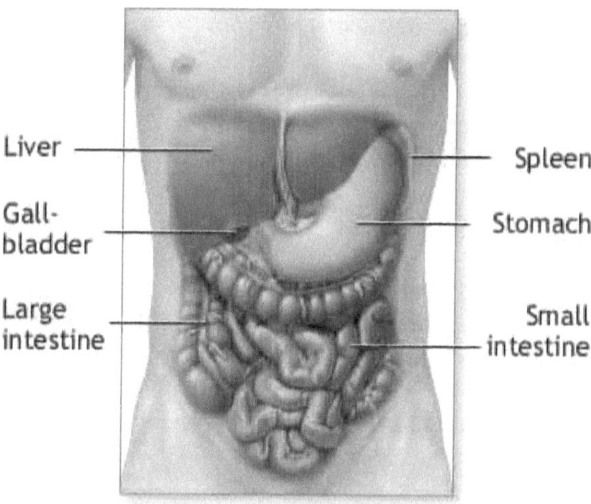

Relax

When you blush, you can quickly help fade the redness by relaxing your muscles, particularly in your shoulders and neck. Try to let go of the tension that you are suddenly holding.

In order to relax, try:

- Remembering to breathe in and out (deeply if you can).
- Reminding yourself that this isn't the first time you have blushed and it probably won't be the last time. This can be oddly comforting.
- Smiling. Smiling may help as our cheeks naturally redden when we smile; smiling also helps us feel happier, which may destroy any social anxiety.

It's all about the breathing. I swear by 4, 7, 8. Not just for stressful situations, even for getting to sleep. You inhale deeply through your nose for a count of 4; hold your breath for a count of 7 and then exhale, slowly and steadily, through your mouth for a count of 8.

What is 4-7-8 breathing? *"The single best anti-anxiety method I've found"* - Dr. Weil.

Although the anti-anxiety calming effects of this exercise can be experienced immediately the real power of this technique comes with regular daily use, at least twice a day, over 8 weeks says Dr. Andrew Weil. By practicing these deeper rhythms voluntarily, we create more effective involuntary patterns of breath integrating the physiological effects into our daily lives. With enough practice, you should begin breathing more deeply without having to give it any extra thought.

Ibuprofen

The flush that develops during whole-body heat stress depends partly on prostaglandins production in the skin. Variations in the strength of this local mechanism may contribute to individual differences in susceptibility to blushing and associated anxiety. To investigate this, a study consisted in applying the anti-inflammatory agent ibuprofen (which blocks prostaglandins formation) topically to a small area of the cheek in 16 participants with a fear of blushing and in another 14 without this fear.

Changes in skin blood flow were monitored at the ibuprofen-treated site and at a mirror image control site while participants sang (to induce embarrassment and blushing) and during aerobic exercise (to induce flushing).

The topical ibuprofen treatment inhibited increases in cheek blood flow in both groups during both of these tasks.

These findings suggest that prostaglandins contribute to dilatation of facial blood vessels both during emotional arousal (embarrassment) and aerobic exercise.

Furthermore, fear of blushing may be associated with mechanisms that delay the resumption of normal vascular tone after a period of vasodilatation.

As topical ibuprofen gel is associated with only minor side effects (*Massey et al., 2010*), it may be suitable both for intermittent and long-term use as an aid for blushing control. In particular, knowing that ibuprofen suppresses blushing might help people who are frightened of blushing engage in social encounters that they otherwise would have avoided. This could provide an opportunity to habituate to anxiety-provoking cues and allow the fear of blushing to subside.

Antihistamines

There may be a high likelihood that most people with this condition have histamine intolerance. The symptoms of histamine intolerance can show during different activities where your heart rate increases or when blood rushes to your skin. **Normal people don't have the "blush rash" reaction as a result of this common phenomena. Normal people have lower histamine levels which do not irritate the skin when more blood rushes**. If you have high histamine level, your histamine will attack your skin cells and react by becoming inflamed. **Try taking a non-drowsy antihistamine a few times and see whether you have a lesser effect**.

I think it is a shame that most of the people with this condition believe that they have severe anxiety problems. They don't, they just have a unfortunate symptom that reacts to anxiety along with other blood pressure increasing attacks such as stress, working out. Talk to your doctor about it.

"For some people, exercise can cause the cells in the skin to release histamine, which in turn can cause the blood vessels to widen, adding to the exercise-induced flushing," says Dr. Adam Friedman, associate professor of dermatology at the George Washington University School of Medicine and Health Sciences. In extreme cases, this could even lead to a form of hives, he says.

For those who may have extreme flushing due to the release of histamine, some antihistamine drugs like Cetirizine may help douse the cutaneous flames if you take it before exercising (talk with a dermatologist if it's stressing you out.)

H2 Histamine Receptors = Stomach
H1 Histamine Receptors = Skin and Blood Vessels

Stimulation of H1 in blood vessels causes vasodilation which causes the redness in inflammation.

H-1 receptors are present in capillary resistance vessels. H1-receptor stimulation gives dilation of the precapillary vessels and a redness/swelling of tissue.

Testimonial

"I get VERY red-faced too. I read in SHAPE that taking an **antihistamine** before exercise helps... and I personally think it does help."

Diet

If you notice that when you fast from food and the face becomes less red, it is probably related to the digestive system. When you wake up after a night of no eating, is the face less red? I've seen so many others talk about doing crazy diets, etc. and if you think about it, it has probably impacted rosacea to some degree because they are getting more nutrients and more fiber naturally but if we just make sure our colon is clean we probably have more flexibility and have less impacts on the skin.

1st testimonial

"<u>Since my change in diet, by eliminating wheat, dairy, corn, cottonseed and canola oil, soy and hormone farm/red meats - my anxiety has disappeared</u>. Each day is calm, cool, relaxed, my skin feels extraordinary - not hot and clammy - and my clothes feel so nice on my skin. The THING?? is gone. Whatever it was that was 'wrong' seems to be gone now. Yet, nothing has changed, save for my diet. And - if you have the fear of craving these foods after getting rid of them - an interesting thing I noticed. Once you are off these drug-foods, you no longer miss them.

My anxiety came from food intolerances and from my intestines. My blood pressure is excellent, and I only use propranolol now for big public speaking events (over 70 or 80 people)..."

2nd testimonial

"I take probiotics and enzymes that help to break down the food that I eat. I notice that my hands don't get cold anymore. I have just started to increase my uptake of fiber. Thanks so much for that tip. Things are starting to change. Thanks everybody for all your tips/suggestions. God bless you all!"